maija grotell

Works Which Grow From Belief

Jeff Schlanger & Toshiko Takaezu
Studio Potter Books

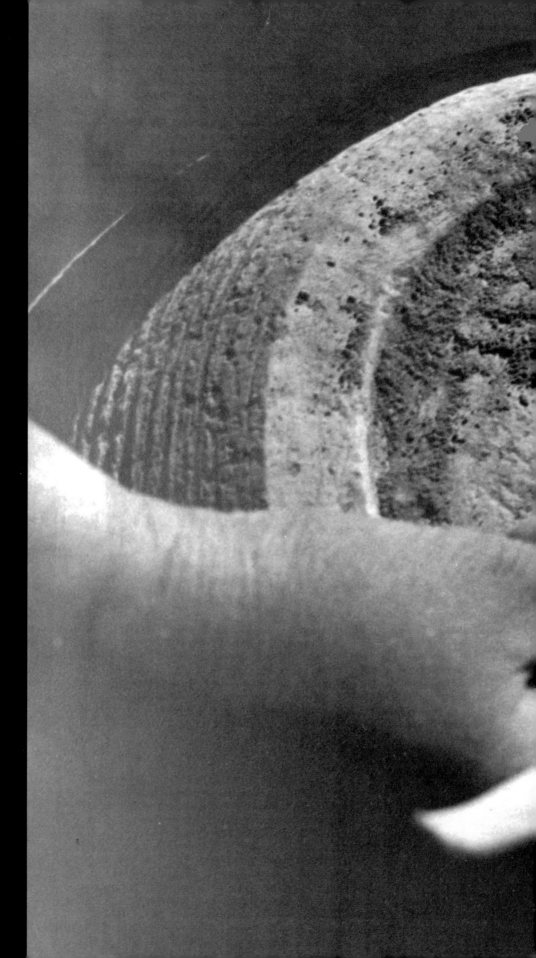

A STUDIO POTTER BOOKS
MONOGRAPH

GERRY WILLIAMS, EDITOR

Designed by Eismont Design,
Richmond, New Hampshire.

Library of Congress Cataloging-
in-Publication Data.

Schlanger, Jeff, 1937–
Maija Grotell: works which grow
from belief / Jeff Schlanger &
Toshiko Takaezu. – 1st ed.
p.   cm.
Includes bibliographical references.
1. Grotell, Maija – Criticism and
interpretation. 2. Grotell, Maija. –
Interviews. 3. Potters – United
States – Interviews. 4. Pottery –
20th century – United States.
I. Takaezu, Toshiko. II. Title.
NK4210.G755S36 1996
738'.092–dc20   96-17478

ISBN 0-9652176-2-0

Printed at the Stinehour Press,
Lunenburg, Vermont.

Cover: *Maija Grotell's Chinese
cotton studio smock. Photograph by
Al Karevy. Page 1: Maija Grotell's
wheel at Cranbrook ceramics studio.
Photograph by John Pickel.
Frontispiece: Opalescent Sphere,
1953, 15 x 13 ½", American Craft
Museum 1967.12. Photograph by
Eva Heyd. Pages 4-5: Maija Grotell
signing the foot of one of her pots.
Photograph by Harvey Croze.*

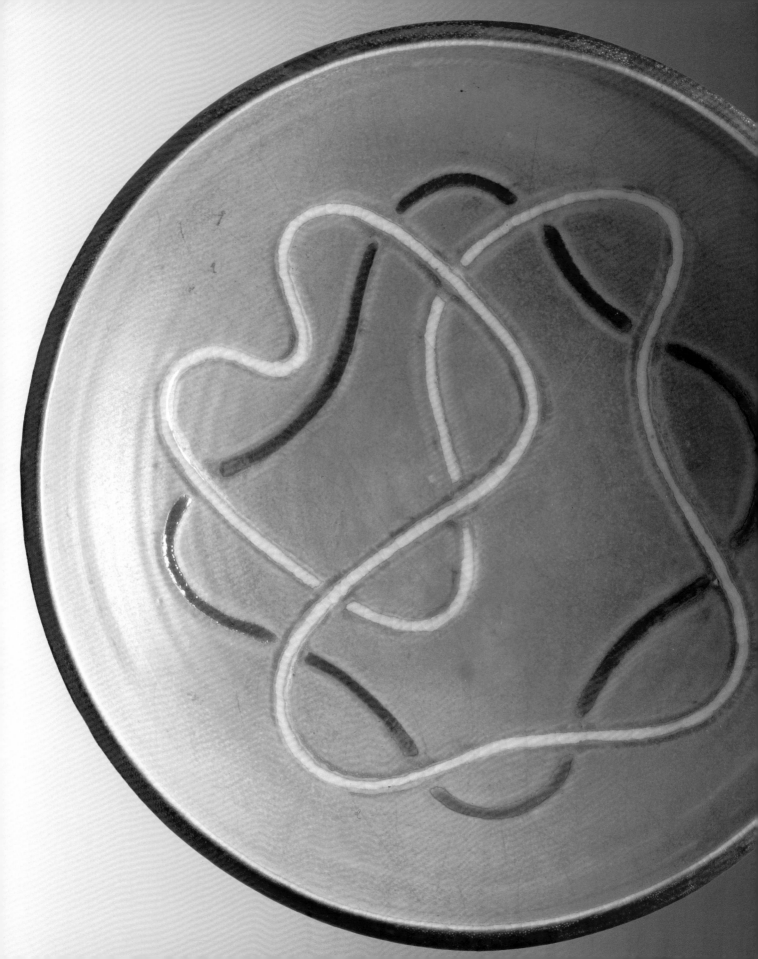

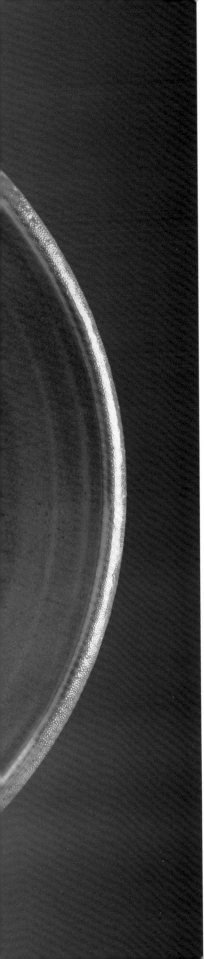

MAIJA GROTELL:
WORKS WHICH GROW FROM BELIEF

Development of an elemental creative statement is an awesome achievement. Most great pottery has grown out of accumulations of technical and aesthetic refinements by generations of workers within a traditional style. Maija Grotell worked independently, in the middle of America, during a time when each element of her art had to be perfected from within her own experimental ingenuity and powerful spirit.

She was one of a few modern artists — Brancusi, Mondrian, Gaudi — who lived a life in such a dedicated way as to be able to create a culture of Belief.*

Works which grow from Belief are never, even at the beginning, only personal statements. They rise from the inspired identification of a unique soul with the possibilities of structure and material. They relate materials to gravity, which is their message for our posture. They breathe and vibrate with vision. They strike a timeless balance between protection and freedom. Their clarity comes from an exact knowledge of human spaces in relation to the scale of the world.

These are the works which are always relentlessly modern. They are the products of a powerful, sustained series of human acts which expose basic patterns of growth. These real discoveries radiate fresh pride and solid optimism, revealing a tangible totality of human perception.

Each of Maija Grotell's prime works is a unique focus of the universal language of form known as pottery. And in these works, every element of this language has been brought to a point of development worthy of the best works of any time or place.

THE LIFE

Today, looking across the waters of New York harbor, it may not be a simple thing to imagine the America to which Maija Grotell came, an immigrant from Finland, in 1927. Ceramics facilities in the United States when she arrived bore little resemblance to the proliferating resources we take for granted at the end of the century. Now we choose from among educational programs on all levels. Suppliers and manufacturers offer ready-mixed clays and glazes, power equipment, every size and type of kiln, plus dozens of magazines, hundreds of informative books, and millions of color slides.

Ceramics in the nineteen-twenties in America tended to be considered either an industry or a hobby. The global history of ceramic art and its continuity into the present moment had yet to be widely understood. A foundation for the development of this understanding was accomplished, in large part, by the pioneer teaching of Maija Grotell's generation. For them, ceramics practice demanded mastery of the kick wheel and of often difficult, underscaled firing facilities, along with the continuous experimental production of test glazes in order to build a common working knowledge of the possibilities.

The Finland that Maija Grotell was born into, on August 19, 1899 in Helsingfors, was even more stringent an environment. There she had been trained in painting, sculpture and design at The Ateneum, the Central School of Industrial Art, and had completed six years of graduate work in ceramics while supporting herself drawing for the National Museum and working as a textile designer. Ceramic materials, however, were not then available to individuals in Finland, and there was but one teaching job in the entire country. In order to continue to develop her individual work, she had to leave.

Maija's first summer in America was spent at the State College of Ceramics at Alfred, New York, where she met, among others, the founder of the school, Charles F. Binns, and Arthur Baggs of Ohio State University, leaders in the establishment of university-level ceramics programs where the art of clay was offered as adjunct to established engineering curricula. Maija had already found work at the Inwood Studios in Manhattan and went on to teach at Union Settlement and then at the Henry Street Settlement, while exhibiting and selling her own ceramics. From 1936 to 1938 she was also the first art instructor at the School of Ceramic Engineering at Rutgers University, New Brunswick, New Jersey.

A Diploma from the 1929 Barcelona International Exposition and a Silver Medal at the Paris International in 1937 were among the first of twenty-five major exhibition awards she was to receive over the next thirty years, including six from the Syracuse Ceramic National Exhibitions and the Charles Fergus Binns Medal from Alfred University in 1961.

In the fall of 1938 she was invited to enter a very different creative environment when she joined architect Eliel Saarinen, sculptor Carl Milles, weaver Marianne Strengell and later designer Charles Eames on the faculty of Cranbrook Academy of Art, outside Detroit, Michigan. It was while teaching at Cranbrook that she achieved her finest series of works. Her work was purchased for twenty-one museum collections, including the American Craft Museum and the Metropolitan Museum of Art in New York, the Detroit Institute of Arts, the Art Institute of Chicago, the Everson in Syracuse, the Cleveland Museum of Art and the Cranbrook Academy of Art Museum. Her extensive glaze research enabled Eliel and Eero Saarinen to use huge exterior walls of brilliantly colored glazed brick in the architecture of the General Motors Technical Center. She died in 1973.

Indications of the sources of Maija Grotell's fulfillment are in many areas of her life story: the caliber of the people she knew in Finland and America, the range of her training, and the exceptional consistency of the rhythm of her life. Her mother had been an artist, and A.W. Finch, her teacher at the Ateneum, was also a painter with broad experience in the Parisian art world of the time. She was trained to be a professional in every branch of fine and industrial art, along with students such as Toini Muona who later became important figures in Finnish design. At Cranbrook, her colleagues had international reputations and were at work on major projects in all fields.

Maija Grotell, trained to be independent, knew six languages, which may be one reason why her work is so clear and free from colloquialism. As a girl she was an exceptional athlete and had accustomed herself early to demanding high standards of strength and endurance from her body. Later, she taught herself to throw large, perfectly centered vases using more than fifty pounds of clay on a stand-up, foot-operated wheel after making and wedging all the clay by hand. She was also a full-time teacher and a full-time potter.

She said, in 1968, "I worked 'round the clock; all the windows were dark. I felt very fortunate to be able to work all night and then, they not notice in the morning if I had. I worked awfully hard. It's not *wise* to do it in that way. But, I was fortunate to be so. Oh, ya, that's all right. I was just lucky the way I was."

As a teacher, she offered each student a way into creative art and an individual standard of excellence. With great care for the singular rhythms of each person, she used silence, humor, disarming ambiguity and an occasional, powerfully-focused, perfectly-timed remark delivered in a centered, resonant voice. The exquisite control of her teaching and its lasting inspiration was often suddenly clear years later when a student realized that this teacher, who had the wisdom to direct students to find the sources of their own creative lives, had also renounced the spectacular but short-lived results that can come from teaching techniques and style.

Maija Grotell's commitment communicated belief fully and with great originality. She joined strong friendships with many of her students while maintaining the standards of her own unique vision. She said succinctly, "If you help a student too much they are lost when they leave or you leave. The best thing you can do for students is to make them independent so they do not miss you."

THE WORKS

Maija Grotell's works have great posture. They stand with glory and without arrogance. They are powerful, secure and stable, yet they stand softly. Their backbones grow up from the center of the earth as they inhale, use and warm great volumes. Their breath is deep and controlled by the spiraling power of their curving walls. Their throats are open through to the bottoms of their insides, showing us that the gestures of our interior passages to the outside can be magnificent.

The touch that formed these vessels is confident and powerfully rhythmic. The mark, the pace of the moving hand and strong, propelling foot — tender, irregular and slow — remains in the deep surfaces. The sculptured skin is approachable, and the whole construction of the clay shell shows how beautifully it is possible to handle naturally turning ceramic material.

Maija's shapes bloom from great posture, great breathing and great gesture. The best of them are an achievement of a vision, a yielding of material finally to beautifully continuous human determination.

She said, "I always have something I am aiming at, and I keep on. I do not sketch on paper, I sketch in clay. So if it is not what I want, I make another one and keep on. In that way, I have many similar pieces. My reason is not for repeating, but for improving. Because if I have one that I like — I mean one that has come to what I was aiming at, then it has no interest any more and I would not try to make another one. And also I like to *learn* from each piece I make in *some* way."

Layers of bold pattern and vivid color extend the gesture of spun forms. Pattern drawn in color can be clear and fresh as though it had just grown there. The source is nature — the natural process of building a series of perfect layers, each one alive with authority. Maija Grotell was always curious about materials and their possibilities. "I'm not being curious about my next door neighbor. But about materials I have been *tremendously* curious."

Colored clay slips alone create an extraordinarily rich surface on many pieces. This range of roughness is also used under glazes and sometimes built up in relief patterns. Areas of slips and glazes are brushed onto the works as the wheel revolves so that even deep glazing radiates the handled, spiral skin of the clay beneath.

Maija developed a dazzling series of turquoise blues from copper oxide, as well as reduced reds, plums and flesh pinks. Dark, boiling iron-oxide glazes balance contrasting color patterns to build surfaces of symphonic volume. Pale yellows, greens, tans, grays and white extend a glowing spectrum along with intense accents of orange and silver.

Color of this power is extremely difficult to use; it can destroy the character of form and coat like commercial paint. But Maija Grotell's best works are complete summations. She controls a chorus of color over memorable form, firing her kilns with inspiration to project the clay ground up through the bright layers.

Coordinated and clear, Maija's means were fire, the turning wheel and well-wedged clay. Giving herself meant passing on all passion, patience and belief within the single life she lived. Any writer, even one who also works on the wheel, may not locate Maija Grotell in words, pictures passing on a printed page, or even in the transformation of memory over time. Know her now in a feeling the body receives directly from the pottery. Her pottery, stated in clear joy, full color and fresh, classic form for forty years of powerfully sustained work, remains with us all, holding a whole woman.

Maija's spirit seems to ride the rippling waters of the harbor now, out where you can almost see around the edge of the world and on beyond the moon into deep space. Maija's spirit seems to be a lighted buoy, with an iron bell — essential, steady, and anchored below the shifting tides, deep beneath the undercurrents, tied into the invisible molten center of spinning Earth.

Jeff Schlanger

* EDITOR'S NOTE: belief, n. 1. the state of believing; conviction that certain things are true; faith, especially religious faith. 2. trust; confidence: as, I have belief in his ability. 3. acceptance of or assent to something as trustworthy, real, etc.: as, a claim beyond belief. 4. anything believed or accepted as true. 5. an opinion; expectation; judgement: as, my belief is that she'll come. 6. a creed or doctrine. (Webster's New World Dictionary)

Young Maija.
Photograph courtesy
Margueritte Kimball.

S I S U :
T H E   S P I R I T   O F   S T R U G G L E

I N T R O D U C T I O N

The genesis of this Maija Grotell book was in the bright sitting room of Maija's small apartment at Cranbrook on May 24, 1968. Toshiko Takaezu and I had come to visit Maija in connection with an exhibition of her work at Cranbrook, Syracuse and New York. I was to write an illustrated article that was published in *Craft Horizons* and later in *Form, Function, Finland* titled "Works Which Grow From Belief".

We had with us an early model cassette recorder and were surprised to find Maija eager to speak with us and fully capable of summoning the energy to tell her life story for the first time. Ill, Maija had retired herself from teaching, and her body had become disabled. But when she spoke, that rumbling, powerful voice came rolling on out like her pottery — whole, centered, resonant and indelibly clear as always.

And we laughed together. We also asked many questions and have been thinking about her answers ever since. When Maija spoke, the sound of her words was delivered with a focus, economy and sense of timing that reverberated in the mind of a listener. She had never spoken so many words as she did that afternoon, telling her own story. We had never learned so much about her life and times.

The tapes were transcribed, donated to American Craft Research, and finally edited as it has at last become clear that they contain key words that deserve to be passed on. Maija speaks directly about her own development as an artist and teacher. She sets this development into the era through which she lived, and among the colleagues with whom she had contact. Throughout her story, we sense the strong activity of rhythmic work which permeates the real life of a maker. We also become aware of her personal and artistic independence from the institutions to which she contributed so generously.

But the core of this book is in the album of pictures of Maija Grotell's pottery that has been assembled. None of the pictures gathered here is ideal; they have been taken by many photographers over many years. Printed color is always a compromise. Shots that seem to show the stance of a piece often fail to indicate the depth of its glaze. Nevertheless, it may be evident to the reader that the body of work here presented contains a major contribution to ceramic art.

What you have in your hands, then, could be called the transmission of a blueprint of Maija's way, passed on by two whose lives have been profoundly moved by our meetings together with Maija Grotell and her work, turning still.

It is offered first for the makers — those practicing believers in the process — who always need to know what it really takes to keep going on. We offer all readers exposed to the ever-oncoming electronic revolution an opportunity to go back and renew contact with an ancient standby, a universal tactile human language of the whole person: foot-powered pottery, centered and thrown by hand out of the heart.

CONVERSATION WITH MAIJA GROTELL

AT CRANBROOK — MAY 24, 1968

EARLY LIFE

Jeff Schlanger: Can you say something about how it felt to be working in ceramics in America at a time when very few people were doing that, especially at high temperature, and with almost no equipment, books or information about the process?

Maija Grotell: There was not [any of that] **in Finland either, you see. In Finland when there was something important coming up it was only Elsa Elenius and me and, of course, Professor** [A.W.] **Finch that were invited to participate in international shows. So, it was not very much different.**

At that time, there was just no future. I did not understand when I came over here [to the U.S.A.] **how they ever had a ceramics department there** [in Finland] **because there was only one teaching position — and still is — in the country. This Arabia Factory business was not in sight at that time. It was a fool's paradise to study early. There was no thinking about what to do next, but you always knew you could do something else.**

JS: You must have really wanted to do it, then?

MG: *Yes*. The school gave you a background to do other things. In Finland, it was impossible for anyone to have one's own studio. There was no place you could buy any chemicals or anything like that at that time. I ordered some chemicals from Paris that I wanted to try out, from England, from Germany and from France. But the duty was very high. If it would have been for studio use, real studio use, the government would not have given me permission.

I did not know how they were teaching in this country and I realized that teaching probably would be my livelihood. So I wanted to know how they were teaching here. That was all. I went the first summer to the College of Ceramics at Alfred [New York]. **Professor Charles F. Binns**[1] **was living then and he had these lectures. It was very much like what I had gone through before with Professor Finch in Finland.**

Pages 12-13: *Maija with Universe Jar. Photograph by Charles Eames.* Page 14: *Universe Jar. 1941. 13⁷⁄₁₆ x 14¼". Cranbrook Art Museum, 1952-3. Photograph by Ferdinand Boesch.* Opposite: *Maija's hands with recently wedged clay. Photograph by Harvey Croze.*

It only gave me more assurance than information. That was my aim: to get a little more assurance.

[Alfred] was very regimented at that time. It was more like in any school. You had to do certain things if you wanted it or not. You were not free.

JS: You once told me that Professor Binns used to throw pots in small sectional pieces.

MG: I had bought Professor Binns' book in Finland (*The Potter's Craft*, Van Nostrand, 1910, 1922). I ordered it, I think, from England. I have given that book away now. There were really very few books available at the time.

Professor Binns used calipers and used them for two or three sections. He got them just accurate. They fitted perfectly. He was very proud of it. He had a demonstration for us. But, to make one that big (8-10 inches high) took the whole week. I couldn't understand that. They were just all "Oo"s and "Aah"s over it. "Oh, marvelous" when they fitted all together. He did not throw them together. They fitted.

One day, I remember at Alfred, I was not careful or cautious as I went walking through there. I saw a room entirely empty, and just a wheel. I don't remember where I got the clay from. But it was a different wheel from what I had seen before. So, before I knew it, I had a big hunk on the wheel and was throwing there in this empty room, very neat.

And then I felt something funny. And there was Professor Binns in the doorway. I felt it, you see, before I saw him, and I nodded. He came to me and said, "They *do* teach you throwing in Europe, do they not?" I said, "Yes, they *do*." But I felt in the air something different. I did not save the piece. And I did not do it again. I cleaned up and made it neater. I didn't know, maybe it was his own room. I didn't know, but I felt resentment there. I had a big piece that I threw.

JS: One piece, you mean.

MG: Yes. All this went on spontaneously. In Finland, there was no planning what you should do next. You enjoyed it for the moment. There at Alfred, also, it was interesting at that time. Old students came back and visited, and Professor Binns introduced them to the group. There I learned to know Professor Arthur Baggs,[2] for example,

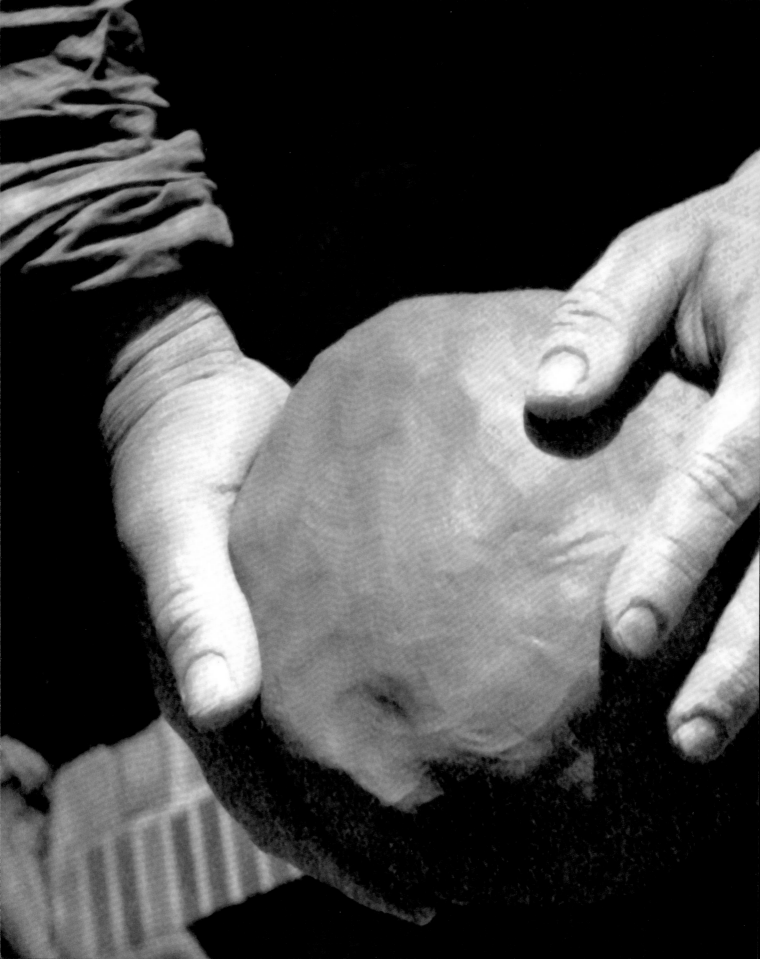

from Columbus, Ohio.   All the people in important positions came at that time.

JS: *Do you feel that there were any people who really understood what you were doing and appreciated it or encouraged you or gave you some kind of support?*

MG: I might be wrong, but I felt that Professor Baggs was one.   I might be over-estimating him, but I don't think so.   I always wanted to be like Professor Baggs.   I don't think he ever did it for an audience or publicity.   He just kept on doing.   He was, I felt, a scientist and an artist combination which was very rare in anyone in this country or anyone else that I knew anywhere.   I had a tremendous respect for him.

I met him only very briefly, so I never knew him really, you see.   He started with the carborundum and the copper reds.   I know Edgar Littlefield and I think he is a wonderful man, but I don't think he would have had that insight as Professor Baggs [had], for example.

It was a piece of copper glaze dropping on a carborundum kiln shelf in the kiln, and it was red.   There have been two writings about it.   One was in 1933 in the *American Ceramic Bulletin*.[3]   And one was later that Littlefield wrote in *Ceramics Monthly*,[4] and I have never seen it mentioned in any books before.

JS: *Is that what you use mostly for copper reds — silicon carbide?*

MG: I have used that, yes.

JS: *Did you also use atmospheric reduction for reds?*

MG: Yes, I have done that, too.   They are all in different processes.

JS: *It seems you've used practically every single ceramic glazing process.*

MG: That's what I mean with that: "I have always been curious."

JS: *Another unique glaze effect is this iron spot glaze — with Albany slip bubbling up through a stiffer light-colored glaze. You did a whole series of magnificent pieces with big, flowing bubbles and also very delicate ones. Do you remember how you started with that?*

MG: I had never seen it done before.

JS: *Did you try to do it from scratch, or did you run across some apparent accident in the kiln that you could work on?*

MG: No. But, *most* of my pieces are one layer on top of another layer. And how I started with that I remember. In Finland I had a genuine pearl in a ring — a pearl that I had been diving for myself and found. I thought that it was non-destructible, very strong.

I had it on when I was throwing and everywhere. Then I cracked the enamel on that. It was brown inside and layers and layers, you see. And then I started also with birds — they had layers and layers of feathers, and that made the impression that you had. Then I read in some natural history magazines here on skin — how many layers it is in just the surface skin to make that translucency. So I felt that everything has to be layers and layers if it is good. If it gets depth, it's because everything in nature is layers and layers. And in the grass it's layers and layers.

JS: In the blade of grass.

MG: Yah. So, almost all my pieces are one layer on top of another layer. And, of course, manganese or iron has the explosive quality. It boils. And manganese does it more than iron. So, I felt that if the top glaze is stiff enough and the iron is strong enough to pull through — that was how it came.

JS: And it probably took a while before you were able to use it.

MG: Oh, yes. And what I did in the beginning was, that I wanted to use them on thinner and smaller pieces. But the explosion there with the iron pulling through the other glaze cracks the piece. I don't know how many I had crack. I mean hundreds of them.

And then the students here at Cranbrook were so anxious to use it. They wanted to use it. They could not take the disappointment.

I had one man coming here in the summer school. And he came in and raved about that he had so many *orders* on these that he came to Cranbrook to learn how. He did not get one sample. I told him how. But, of course, I did not care for this taking orders on something that somebody else could make money on if it was possible. Fortunately, in the class was one man that probably got a little suspicious of me, that I gave him the wrong steer. So, he wanted to learn it, too. And every sample he made came out beautifully. The other one could not get

them — only when I was holding his hand. I felt sorry for him; but only when I was just next to him and said "One more layer," and so forth, not just telling him and walk away but just standing over him.

JS: You have a very strong point of view about what you feel ceramics can do. Often people seem to talk about pottery as if it were either just functional ware, production-made inexpensively for sale — or, on the other hand, as a non-functional object, just an expression — often a very romantic expression. There was a different feeling here. It was almost like pottery itself was a fine art — the equal of any other kind of art.

MG: I was fortunate to have that understanding at Cranbrook because of Mr. Eliel Saarinen.[5] He was very sensitive to things. He might not have understood them quite. For example, a man came and wanted to place an order for a dozen bowls and so on. I said, "I'm sorry, I have not the time to take your order." And he got mad, furious. He said, "I bring you a good order and I will bring you more afterwards and you refuse. I will have you fired."

And he went to find Mr. Saarinen. And Mr. Saarinen came to me and said, "What *is* the story really about?" I said, "He wanted me to do mass production. And I do not have the time, Mr. Saarinen." "She's right. Go off." And the way he did it was just marvelous.

TEACHING

JS: Can you tell me something about teaching methods?

MG: Most teachers as I knew them and as I watched them, were teaching strictly 'step-by-step.' You know, I just hate the word, but that's what they used. It was just only one way of doing one thing. It really made me sick in even watching them in the way they were teaching — *dum, dum, dum.* I was never taught that way. It was much freer. Professor Finch never worked in that way, you know — strict. He let us try things out.

JS: I think you once told me that in the beginning when you were teaching at Cranbrook, you used to give more direction to your students than you did later on.

MG: Because we had to have some start. The students in the beginning — very few of them were creative students. We had no scholarships and they really had to have money to come to Cranbrook.

JS: *You had said that everybody praised you for the quality of the student work, and that you felt that you had put much of your own energy into their creations.*

MG: One student, for example, that I had the first year here, was a very poor sculptor and in some way came to pottery. I felt sorry for him and I helped him a great deal. He directly copied me. So, it was not good for *him*.

But teaching, I think, you don't see it just when you do it. You see it first later on. If you help a student too much, they are lost when they leave or you leave. So I do not believe in that. I would not do it again because he [the sculptor] never did anything. He was too dependent on me just helping him. And so it was with many in New York. I think the best thing you can do for students is to make them independent, instead of dependent, so they do not miss you when you leave. I know I had helped many in New York. But, when I helped them, they got their work in magazines and so forth.

JS: *When I was a student at Cranbrook in 1956, I didn't understand it at that time. It took me several years after I left to begin to understand what had happened over the year I was here. There was a tremendous amount of teaching going on even though it was not directed teaching. You never told me how to make glazes or how to throw pots or how to do anything. But you taught a great deal — I see now — about just how the whole thing goes together. You were conscious of all that, I'm sure, of how you talk to people even though you are not telling them specifically what to do.*

MG: I had many students. (I don't mean you, now.) But to do the best for them I had to be very *careful*. One woman, when I came within a yard's distance from the wheel, I could feel a very *explosive circle* there. I was afraid of disturbing it in any way. She killed herself afterward — ten or fifteen years after she had been at Cranbrook. She came visiting me just three weeks before she did it. I made her feel very good on that visit; so I was glad, that I was not in any way...She was amazed that I knew her father was an important educator and amazed over many things I brought up just to make her feel good.

They had lost money in some way and she was afraid she would not have enough to live on. And I said, "Heavens! You are lucky. Nothing is more fun than to earn your own living." [Laughter] Then, she spoke about that she had been thinking of being an architect. I said, "Isn't it wonderful. You could really do anything you wanted to."

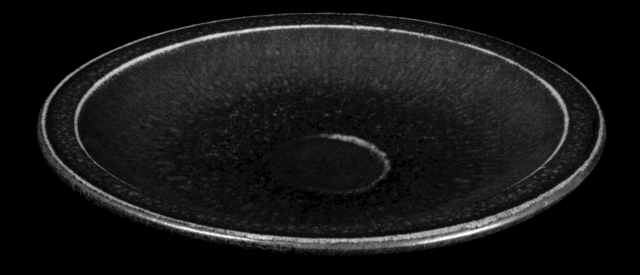

She was always a very intelligent and gifted girl. But very emotional in that way. It was interesting, though, that I would feel that tension around her and have to be always very careful.

JS: How did you feel about teaching in general? You were also stacking kilns and doing all kinds of other studio work. You said you worked tremendously long hours.

MG: I enjoyed teaching very much at that time. I would not enjoy it today because I feel that I would not have the energy quite that it takes to do it well. I enjoyed it *very* much. Being in this country — an immigrant — all my friends came from my students. I really enjoyed it in many, many ways.

Of course, the teaching took energy from one. One thing also, if I had something on my mind and was excited about it, I felt it was better to try to keep it to myself and not just blurt it out, because even my best students got influenced by that, you see. And it was not good for them. I wanted them to be themselves. I was surprised when I sometimes noticed it in some of my very gifted students that I'd been blurting out about something I had on my mind and wanted to do. It was not good for *them*.

ELIEL SAARINEN

JS: Can you say a little about the work you did for Eliel and Eero Saarinen on the architecture of the glazed brick colored walls at the General Motors Technical Center?

MG: That happened in this way. I had been firing all night long — I never left the kiln. I had missed breakfast because the kilns kept on going. I came out from the studio on a Sunday morning.[6] There I met Mr. Eliel Saarinen all laughing. I had given him one of these bowls with this red glaze inside. And he said, "Can you glaze bricks with that color that I have in the bowl?" Well, I felt that was disgusting. I said, "No!"

But then, when I had a *little* rest after this, I felt Mr. Saarinen did not mean it in that way. But I will find some lowfire samples and put them in an envelope and say that these can be fired on brick. That's how it started. Then, they brought me bricks and bricks and bricks in the pottery and I had to glaze them all in the colors they wanted.

JS: Were they used commercially?

MG: Then, they contacted the factory and the engineers said no glaze would be right for building outside in this weather. So the Saarinens put all these hundreds of bricks that I had glazed outside in the snow. I told Mr. Saarinen that I could not be responsible for that if they even last one winter. They might not last two winters. They had engineers here where Eero Saarinen had his studio, and they wanted me in on that conversation. I felt that I had not the time. But I had given them all the recipes I had used and all the directions. But then they had many engineers and many students from Ohio State to work on the glazes. I did not work on the final glaze. But I showed it could be glazed on brick.

JS: Do you know if your glazes stood up over time when they tested them?

MG: There is only one color they have had to replace, one color only. I don't remember what color it was. It was one wall that did not stand up very well. I think it was a cobalt if I remember right. I don't know why. It's now all over. They use it on any building.

JS: Did you ever get any compensation for the work you did on that?

MG: No. No. I asked Eero how much money I could spend on this. "Fifty dollars." I think it was more. I think the firing [was] extra. But I did not get any for that. If I would not have done that, the engineers really did not want to do it. Architects, you see, when you work with architects in general, they are very impatient. They want it right away like a pancake. They had to build a new factory for this.[7] Opening day was so and so and it all had to be finished. Some other architects from General Motors came, and they wanted flowerpots.

JS: For you to make by hand?

MG: Yes. Ornamental. Well, they would have needed and wanted as many as I could do. I made several. I did not make more than ten or so. The students, if they had something suitable, they worked on that. I could not turn the whole department over for General Motors. We did a great deal for them.

JS: You had gotten established at Cranbrook. It's a unique situation at any time to have many important creative people working at one place in an institution really devoted to fine art in all fields. Do you feel that this had any effect on your work?

MG: *No*. I didn't. Professor Saarinen was very much around. He wanted my pieces displayed. I had to have shelves for that. He also showed interest in certain things more than in others. This kind — I could never keep away from him.

JS: This is the piece with the blue ground and the platinum over it.

MG: Well, you see at that time it was so much chrome in the interior, and so it fit the interior. And this was the type of piece that I would not send to Syracuse [Ceramic National Exhibition]**; but, it went well with the interior at that time, with the chrome.**

JS: It looks very beautiful now.

MG: It is in the library here. I did not make it for the library. But, when I had it and Professor Saarinen came around, he wanted it. And we put some other pieces that I made with the platinum, also [there]**. And he wanted them also.**

JS: Will you say something about what you feel the difference is between this kind of work that you thought was more for interiors and your major pieces?

MG: I don't mean I dislike these. I like the black and white. It was also more for interior, but not for a ceramic show.

***Today*, I think, the standards are different. Like Voulkos paints in oil paint if he has not a coloring glaze. So I don't know how I would feel today, if I would have made it today, in sending it to a ceramics show, because the standards are different. At that time, it was, I felt, more for showing your skill in the material, in glazes and in throwing and, well, exhibiting your *knowledge* more or less. I feel this again goes well with that age furniture, and so forth.**

JS: It still looks beautiful. There's something very elemental about it. The decoration isn't at all ornate. It seems very pure somehow. Can you say anything about the design?

MG: I like the design. I made one more with the same design and a white glaze. The design was raised white and semi-opaque glaze over

it, and that's in the Toledo Museum. Also, I used porcelain grog in these. They're white specks I felt was softening and joining the design a little more.

JS: *Then you knew from the beginning that you were going to use platinum on the piece. Do you have any feelings about where the design came from? Did you make drawings for them?*

MG: No, I would not know. But I felt it followed the form.

JS: *There's something in it almost about birds and the sunlight to me because they fly over the surface of the pot somehow. One of the reasons it's still so good is there is a great dimension to the piece. It's not just severe decoration applied to a spherical form. They float and fly over and around the form.*

MG: I think about design *this* way: my designs — I do not want them to be *applied* designs. I want it to *grow from the piece*. That's my aim, at least. And not stuck on, because I feel it should grow from within.

THROWING

JS: *Can you tell me something about the throwing? These are very large pieces, many of these spherical pieces; and there were very few people doing large thrown pieces at that time.*

MG: That was on a treadle wheel. *All* my pieces are in one piece.

JS: *You must have taught yourself after a certain point to make these large pieces — taught yourself throwing.*

MG: Yes. I remember one piece that I made first, one big one. I had not my own studio. It was here at Cranbrook. My hands were bleeding awful. So I went to town and bought gloves — because people just screamed when they saw this and brought more people to see me throwing. They [the gloves] just split in two. I had three kinds that I tried. But you know, the next piece was nothing at all. I had learned how to touch the clay so it did not do that.

JS: *What were people's reactions to seeing one woman by herself all of a sudden doing work of much greater scale than what people were accustomed to?*

MG: Some people had been told about it. They came to Cranbrook and just wanted me to demonstrate a one-hundred-pound piece —

to throw it. I said, "It takes at least a day to wedge the clay for that piece and I cannot." Some of the students tried, too, to do it. Well, I enjoyed doing it. It was not for show. I would have liked to have had a room where I could have worked by myself but I did not have it at that time. I remember once I had to make a flywheel. I made one for myself. I was just all ready; the room was empty and I thought I would do some things now. In came one person. "Oh, you're working." And out again. And then there was a whole crowd of people around me. I had not even elbow space. And I said pointedly, "I think I could work better in Grand Central Station in New York because there people would have somewhere to go." [Laughter] They did not. I said, "I need elbow space." But then, I had to do something that I knew how, I could not work freely. But I did something that I knew exactly so I would not slip in any way.

JS: Did you start the really large pieces after you got to Cranbrook?

MG: I must have, according to the year 1940. In the first year I don't think I did anything. I had to make the studio in order.

JS: Was it difficult for you to find a clay that would work well on a large scale?

MG: I don't remember anything being complicated. Nothing was complicated at that time, that *age*.

JS: You felt that you knew what you wanted and just went and did it.

MG: Yes. I remember only that there were two big, big pieces that I had to make for the New York World's Fair and Oh, gosh, I had not clay enough. I heard too late.

A I M

MG: Before I came here I had studied the map of New York thoroughly for a whole year, and the subways. So, they were suspicious of me because they felt that…

JS: You should be more helpless.

MG: When they said an address, I would go, "Oh, yes." It was nothing

at all. I knew the subway trains. I don't remember how it was, but my family sent me a big bouquet of roses. Oh, gosh, they really could not understand. They told me where to go [to get the roses] and I knew exactly, just because I had worried about it — that I would not [know]. I only got lost in Brooklyn sometimes, but not Manhattan.

JS: *Everybody gets lost in Brooklyn.*

MG: I always have something I am aiming at, and I keep on. I don't sketch on paper, you see, I sketch in clay. So if it is not what I want, I make another one. And keep on. In that way I have many similar pieces. My reason is not for repeating but for improving. Because if I have one that I like, that has come to what I was aiming at, then, it has no interest anymore. I would not try to make another one.

And also, I like to *learn* from each piece I make, in *some* way. It's often *very* complicated to get the shape for the design you have in mind. I have the design in mind and the expression I want to do and I do not get the shape. And then, I have a big piece there that I thought for that design but, obviously, it is not right. I hate to throw it out. So, I quickly have to dream up a new design for the piece. So, they are made in different ways.

JS: *You've had this great feeling for these massive, globular pieces. As far as I can see, it's an original shape. Do you remember how you came to start doing these?*

MG: Do you know, I have always felt it was not an easy thing to do. To get it in the right proportions. I felt it was always a *challenge,* you see.

JS: *In addition to the size and the form, the throwing is very unusual. It's even unusual now, when so many people have power wheels.*

MG: It all goes back, you see. I did a tremendous lot of skiing, skating, swimming and jumping. So all that builds up this desire to do things in that way, I think. You know, to have the strength.

JS: *It's strength and a great deal of independence because you did it alone.*

MG: I felt always at that time that I could run faster than most people except professionals; I could jump higher than most people except professionals. So I was never afraid. I went anywhere. I felt, "I can beat you."

Bowl. 1949. 6½ x 9½".
Iron spot with copper red interior.
Cranbrook Art Museum, 1949.3.
Photograph by Dirk Bakker.

JS: You've set your own standards as far as glazes and throwing and form — all these things. You completely overcame all the obstacles of technical problems and the lack of information. It didn't seem to matter to you that none of it came easily. It didn't seem to stop you at all.

MG: I feel I sometimes go a little too far in that direction. But I am pleased that I accomplished something that is difficult. For example, these with the white glaze with the Albany slip and the red inside. That was a difficult thing to do. But I kept on doing it just because it *was* difficult. And never any promise that it would come out.

JS: Another basic shape you use a lot is a strong bowl form with a high, wide, strong foot. You have perfected that. And, again, it's an original. How did that start?

MG: I remember it was a little amusing, I think. I used to teach in high heels and so forth, in New York. And one other studio — I try to keep the names off — always made very tiny and elegant vases. I made them always wide and said this is "low-heeled" pieces. That was in New York. They said, "They say your pieces are clumsy." "Oh, no, they are not clumsy," said I. [Laughter] This was only just in fun.

JS: How did you learn to make these colors — the turquoise and all the other kinds of colors you used? Were they all solutions you taught yourself?

MG: Yes. It's through *thinking,* really, and through, of course, former experience. When you think about that, then you think, "Well, this *might* come out right." I had three glazes with orange: one was chrome, one was uranium, and one was iron, and they were all the same color. I'm not especially interested in chrome. But I'm very curious about materials, you see. I've always been very curious. I'm not curious about my next door neighbor. But about material I have been *tremendously* curious. I enjoy making samples and correcting them.

WORKING

JS: Was there anyone to help you with the glaze work?

MG: No, no, no, never. But I was fortunate to have one student coming here, and he stacked the electric kiln. But I fired it. He stacked it for me and that was a great help. Otherwise it took a whole weekend,

just the firing and stacking of a kiln, and that was heavy work with that big kiln. I could have made many big pieces instead of doing that.

Usually, the stacking of kilns in most places, it's not considered anything. It just goes. You are paid for teaching, but not for stacking kilns, and there is the heavy work, really.

JS: In addition to the teaching and the stacking of the kilns, you did all the work on the glazes, many at three different temperatures or so.

MG: I worked round the clock. I used to always try to get home before anyone got up so I could take a bath and put a clean blouse on and so forth. They were all dark — all the windows, and I felt very fortunate to be able to work all night, but then, they not notice in the morning if I had. It's not *wise* to do it in that way. But I was fortunate to be so. Oh, ya, that's all right. I was just lucky that way I was.

TRAINING

JS: How long was your training in Finland?

MG: This is interesting. Mother really tried to teach me to be very independent. So when I was ten years old she asked me, "What school do you want to go to?" I did not know the schools, but I said this school that was far away from home. I could not get home, only Christmas and summer holiday. My cousins were there, so I knew the school from that. That was six years.

The four years at Ateneum, the school for arts and industry. You had to have painting, life drawing, everything — perspective. I had sculpture a great deal. They trained one in these four years so you were not specialized in anything; but, you could go and be assistant to an architect or a furniture designer. Or you could do textile designs. So it was all-round training, not specialized. Then, after that you could specialize — post-graduate work. I was six years after that.

Then I did only ceramics. At the same time, I had a job at the biggest and oldest hand-weaving studio that they had — a textile studio. I did rug designs.

Earthenware Bowl,
1924. Museum of Applied Arts,
Helsinki, Finland.

JS: Do you remember anything particular about the school you went to?

MG: I never understood why they had the ceramic department at all, now being over here for practical reasons, because there was only one teaching position in the whole country.

My professor was A.W. Finch and he was English. And he was a *wonderful* man. He was a wonderful *painter,* also. He was just marvelous. He was a terribly exciting person, very exciting person and he was seventy or so when I was there. His paintings were — just vivid. And he had been studying in Paris and knew all the big people there, working with them and so forth.

He said all kinds of things I will never forget. He said to me, "Remember this: keep away from sick people, old people and poor people." [Laughter] "It's catching," he said. "It's catching.'"
He meant it more…

Toshiko Takaezu: In spirit?

MG: Yes. Some people are that way.

TT: That's right. They could be rich, but still be very poor.

MG: He was all these. He was extremely poor. He lived up in a studio there for painting. He had a wife that did not want to live with him. She was in Paris. You did not sell paintings as you do in this country, you see. So, he was poor and he was sick. [He had arthritis.] But he never showed it.

I was so proud when I happened to go out from school at the same time as he did. He was such a wonderful, handsome person, even seventy. I would walk *with* him in the street. I happened to once walk *behind* him when he did not know I was. We had a long hall there in the school and he had to hold on to the wall because he had difficulty walking. But, that was the only time I saw that.

So he was sick and he was certainly old. [Laughter] But he was so jealous if some of the boys came in and talked to you and were flirting with you a little bit. Oh, he was so furious. I understood what he meant because he didn't mean it just in the way of flirting.

JS: Before you went there [to the Ateneum], did you paint and draw?

MG: Yes. My mother went to art school. There were many teachers, still, that had been my mother's teachers. They did not like *me*.

TT: Why?

MG: Because I was just awful and my mother was just wonderful. And she *was* very wonderful. She did sculpture and wood carving, more in Renaissance style, but still, her own design. My father was a business-man. He died when I was fifteen or sixteen.

JS: Tell us the names of people that were students with you at the school.

MG: There is only one left. She was wonderful. She came to school when I was already post-graduate and just came in when I pleased and did pottery. She has done *wonderful* things.

TT: What is her name?

MG: Muona, Toini Muona.[8] She was just so tiny. She is much bigger in these days. She was just a streak and very vivid and exciting. When she came and saw me, she said, "Do you know I have been thinking about you?" I said, "Oh, have you?" And she said, "I think I can learn to do anything you can do only I forget to have my head going in that way when I throw." [Laughter] And then she said, "What good does it do anyhow!" [Laughter] She was very lively.

JS: Can you think of any other students at school that you admired?

MG: I admired them all. We were a wild group. Believe it or not, it was wonderful. Elsa Elenius was my friend that I lived with. That was the girl who was teaching at the art school after Professor Finch died. Mr. Finch died when I had been just a few years in New York.

There was a house next to the office building just next to the school and around a corner. No one wanted to rent it for offices because it would be taken down that year. So it was some artists who had rented it. We all had rooms in that house. It was just around the corner. Then we had studios and worked there, were painting and so forth. The hallway was a big hallway. We were having exhibitions all the time

Page 44: Bowl. 10¾x8½".
Crackle glaze with copper red
interior and fish pattern.
Collection of Mr. & Mrs. Harvey K.
Littleton. Photograph by Brian
Westveer. Opposite: Jug.
Cranbrook Art Museum, 1995.9.
Photograph by R. H. Hensleigh.

in the hall.   We brought in beds and things, just simple things.   One night Elsa dropped to the floor from some kind of an army couch and she swore, "I was just dreaming that I was dancing with the **Prince of Sweden** and falling into these dumps."

We had a wonderful time there.   It was carefree.   There were three places where you could eat.   Two automats and the university cafeteria.   I always took the same thing, and I was so worried that the waitresses or somebody would notice.   "There she comes again.   Watch her now.   This is what she is going to have!" I did not want that to happen, so, I always went around to one, two, three, then again round.

TT: Maija, what did you pick to eat all the time?

MG: The *best* thing that kept me going without making me sluggish or tired or anything was a piece of the smoked salmon that they call lox.   Jewish people have it a great deal.   On top of that was a piece of dill and one peeled potato.   I don't remember if it was coffee.   I never took desserts.

JS: After your graduate training you said that you couldn't set up a studio in Finland.

MG: That's why I kept on going to art school.   Professor Finch got me a position in England.   But, again, I could not earn money in England. I would have to be invited by the government.   I did not get any invitation from the government.   I had only won a few prizes there in Europe at that time.

JS: In addition to Finnish, Swedish, Russian, German and French, you already spoke English by that time?

MG: I took private lessons in English.   I had a very good instructor first.   She demanded so much homework that I would have had to leave the pottery.   I had not time at all.   I was looking for an English teacher who would go easy on me. [Laughter] I found a beautiful, wonderful girl — younger than I, and she was an English baroness.
She had lived in Russia and left Russia.   She was in Finland giving English lessons, supporting her young brother, her old father and various others. I told her what I wanted.   I went there and we read from a book. I would have learned so much more from the other one, but I would

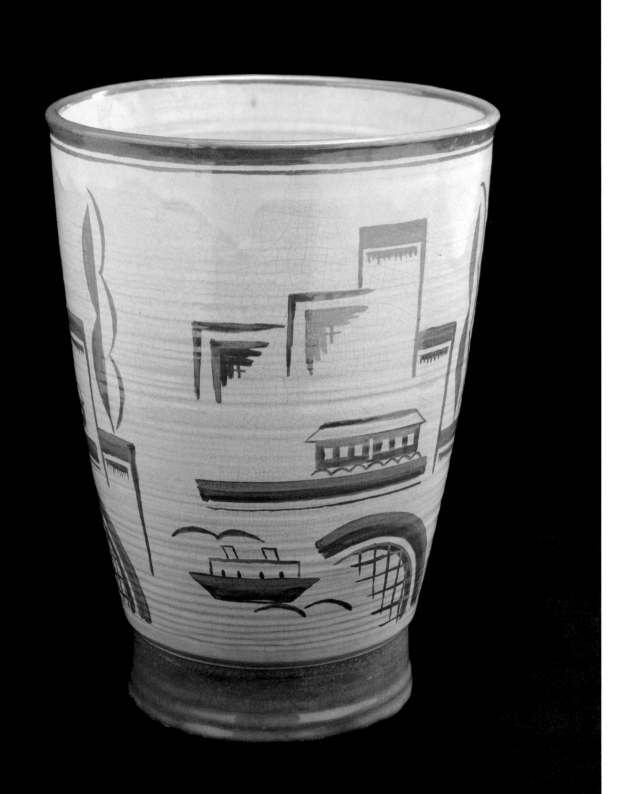

not have had time for pottery or my job either, you see. I was working in the textile studio until five o'clock, and then I did not have dinner or anything. I just went directly to the school and took a train home.

JS: How did you come to take a job in the United States?

MG: There was no other place. In Europe you were not able to get a job or support yourself. So, this country was the only country left, as far as I knew.

JS: So you could continue to do pottery?

MG: Yes. After three days in New York, just with the phone, I had a job. I had not any previous contacts, no. It was the Inwood Studios. It was up in the north tip of Manhattan, where the Hudson and Harlem Rivers meet. And it is not there any more. It was quite a long way from 207th Street & Broadway — that was the last [subway] stop at that time. [It was] a long walk through the woods, to get to the studio.

The first morning when I woke up, they had already gone to the studio. There was a man grinning at me with gold teeth. Oh, I got scared! He was an Indian and he helped with certain things around there. He was very friendly and very wonderful when you knew him. But, I had never seen an [American] Indian before and never one with gold teeth. [Laughter] But we became very good friends.

One year I was there. They wanted me to stay longer, but I said that I'd rather *die* than stay here one more year. [Laughter] First they brought me a long list of things I should do for the day. Well, I put it on the wall and started it. But, she never even let me start with the list. She always brought me other things to do. I was just worried about these things that never got started even.

They made Indian designs and I had to do that. I couldn't do anything at all individually. It was only a beautiful place and interesting people coming there for classes.

Grotell

I'd been two weeks in New York when I was invited to a cocktail party at the Hotel New Yorker. That was one very wonderful world. You see, all I knew about cocktails was these fruit cocktails. [Laughter] I was so happy that somebody else liked cocktails. I was just joyous. I was just jumping to say that I was invited to a cocktail party. It was Prohibition then at that time. I could see it was not pleasing them, so I stopped talking and raving. [Laughter] I thought they were jealous. Heavens, I was invited to a cocktail party and they were not.

I was just waiting for these big bowls of fruit coming in. And I had a little glass to drink something. Then, when I came away from there and came upon these that I had been bragging to about the party, they asked me, "Well, how was the cocktail party?" I said, "Oh, all right. But something went wrong with the cocktails. We just had something little to drink." [Laughter] I remember that so well, so funny.

TT: There was a girl at the cocktail party?

MG: Yes. She was a girl from Georgia — I don't remember what her name was exactly. But she was fascinating. She was tall, black, dark hair, wavy and she had yellow eyes like a tiger. I've never seen anyone with that. Her southern accent — I just loved the girl. But she was very, very wealthy.

She took care of one of my first shows in New York — my first potter's show. It was at the Potter's Shop. She was the person in charge of that. All that people talked about was her, not my work. But it sold very well. I had two shows at the Potter's Shop.

It was so varied. I had not been here long at Inwood when there was a New York Ceramic Society opening and I was supposed to take some of the Inwood products to the exhibition. I took them there and I sat on a chair because I did not get any attention from anyone. There they were arguing if they could take in, if they would fit in such a wonderful show or if they should not be rejected. At that time, you see, pieces were all hand-built and if they were made on the wheel, they were machine-made. They had not seen many potter's wheels. So, I was always to come and teach how you work the machines. I don't know

how many times I've said, "It's not a machine; it's an instrument like
a *piano*." In that way: "It's *not a machine*."

Thinking back, as I said, it was very impractical to study pottery. You
did not have a future with it. When I came to this country, you had to
be rich if you did pottery because there were no positions either. So
it was not as the students now get tremendous salaries, some of them.
It was not a practical profession if you wanted to be just sensible.

You see, it was the Depression. It was very, very hard just to earn a
living in some way. Also the bank holidays. That was all going on in
New York.

HENRY STREET SETTLEMENT

JS: Then you went to Union Settlement?

MG: Union Settlement, yes. I was there only one year because the
director was leaving — a man. He came to me and said that he could
not promise me a job for the following year because he would not be
there. He advised me to find something else.

JS: And then you went to Henry Street Settlement?

MG: Yes. That was very interesting how I got to Henry Street,
because I was highly recommended to King's Park Hospital for World
War I veterans. It was very good pay. I went there and the woman
interviewed me wanted me to sign a contract for fifteen years. I said,
"Is it possible for me to use the studio for my own work when I do not
have classes?" And she said, "Oh, why would you want that? We
nurses and doctors have a wonderful time in the evening." [Laughter]
I said I would not come if I have not permission to work on my own work.
This woman looked exactly like Mae West.

I started early in the morning looking for jobs. They were *not* available,
so I took one week. I had one letter for "Yes" and one letter for "No"
in my pocket. "Yes" and "No" — I knew in which pocket I had these.

I was so tired; I had started early in the morning. I got off at Brooklyn
Bridge and I felt, "Why did I get off here?" There was five cents that
I had lost. Five cents was very important. Why not make use of it in

some way, so I called Henry Street [9] and Miss Canfield that I had met and I had heard that she was very fond of her assistant, and asked her if she had any job for me. "Oh, no," she said, "I do not have a job. But why don't you come and visit me anyhow." I said, "Yes, thank you. I will come."

I had just an envelope, a few photographs from Finland. I'd had one in a Paris exhibition in '33 and that was in a Paris magazine. I have some in German magazines and so forth. That was my introduction, and I showed these. She said, "Oh, I did not know you could do things like these." I said, "I don't think this is so much; I can do more." [Laughter] Anyhow, she hired me that night.

JS: *Had they a pottery studio at Henry Street for a long time?*

MG: They had had it, I think, two or three years. I had been visiting there and I felt that was a dream world. They had a little garden outside the studio. Then I went back to the subway and I called up some friends — I went to a small drugstore — some friends that I knew were, or at least I thought, worried about me. Then, when I went down to the subway, I'd lost my pocketbook. It was really stolen in that drugstore because there were two very ugly men looking at me all the time. I felt uncomfortable. I didn't know anything about anything at that time. I lived in a room at 127th Street. And I walked up to 127th Street.

Well, the sun was coming up but I got home. And I had high heels. I had dressed up for this interviewing and looking, you see, and I had been walking all day. I got to bed and I had a job the following night. But I lost quite a lot of money in that purse because I had not had time to go to the bank and put it in.

JS: *You said it seemed like a beautiful studio to you — Henry Street.*

MG: It was ideal in one way, yes. It was small and had this beautiful little garden outside and one sprinkling birdbath and birds coming there and cats coming there and drinking. It was unusual and it was so peaceful in one way — the garden.

JS: *Was the equipment adequate?*

MG: My first job was to open a kiln that Miss Canfield, the director,

had started. The floor had broken and there were tall pieces and they were all in one, all stuck together. It was a very small kiln and a top-loader.

JS: Do you remember how big it was?

MG: I don't think it was very big, about 20"x20" or 25"x25". It was fired with a torch with oil and air pressure. The pressure you had to pump up. You had to do it by hand. I remember that this torch was the same as they used on the streets for asphalt. It made a tremendous noise and I was scared to death of that kiln.

Then I started to know it a little bit. You know, it was like a human being or a baby; it talked. You knew when it needed more air. You knew when it needed something. It was always talking. It was just wonderful in that way. You put the smokestack on top and out from the window. Then, it got to be too small and we had to have a bigger kiln. We had not room for that. I really missed that one after a while. It was really like a human being.

JS: You had a piece in the Metropolitan Museum that you fired in that kiln?

MG: I think it was fired in that, yes. And I have been trying to find a picture of that piece. It's very clumsy. I made the same design later, but a better shape, on a bigger piece. This, of course, did not go into stoneware — this kiln. It was just low fire. Everything was low fire in New York.

JS: But in Finland you did stoneware?

MG: Some and some porcelain. We had a small kiln for that. But mostly we had a big, big, big kiln that we fired with wood. I think I have done much better here.

JS: Was it difficult to get started in the beginning?

MG: At Henry Street Miss Wald was a very dominating person and she had very specific ideas. She did not like small necks, and I was not allowed to make small necks — only if I was quick enough to hide it when it was made. [Laughter] That made me like to do small necks; but it was forbidden.

I had not much time. I had students. My work at Henry Street in the beginning — I had no salary, but I earned my living with sales. It was a profession. I had to have about two hundred dollars worth of pots ahead to be able to make enough. Then, I said, I had to leave it. That was the only arrangement I could do. I was so worried all the time not to make that money.

JS: Where did you sell the pieces?

MG: At the Potter's Shop, a great deal. Then I had it in many other galleries in town — the Anderson Galleries and the Brummer Gallery.[10] But I did not sell very much there. Then I had it in an awful gallery — what is it called now? Any gallery, except the Potter's Shop, they cheated you. I wish I could remember that gallery's name because it is still there and has branches all over — London, Paris, New York. I would not put one thing in there. At Brummer Gallery when I went there, they had sold a piece two years ago and not paid me. I went there and asked for my money. I had to. I didn't know how I had the time to do that and teaching, too, and stacking kilns and firing kilns. It was just snap, snap, snap.

That was in the beginning. Then, they changed it. I said I would have to leave because I was always so worried that I could not continue. It was too much strain.

RUTGERS

JS: After Henry Street you went to Rutgers?

MG: No. I did them both at the same time because I was asked to Rutgers but it was in the engineering department. Again, Henry Street had gotten a new director. I felt I might not want to stay there long.

So I went to Rutgers. Also, from Rutgers' side, from Professor Brown's side, it was more an experiment, too. Because they were training engineers. But he wanted them to know the process of making a pot by hand. He got very alarmed when one of the students told him he did not want to be an engineer; he wanted to be a potter like Miss

Grotell. [Laughter] **You were not free there in any way. They made the glazes and I had to see what I could do with their glazes. When I asked for something different, they said it could not be done. I knew it could be done; but I could not teach a Rutgers professor!**

What *they* meant by "expert in glazes" was to make them lasting and not crawling. They were dead commercial. I did not care for the greens he made for me. I told him that I would *much* prefer the green from copper than this chrome green. And he snapped at me and said, "Copper cannot be used in highfire. It turns black." Well, I could have shown him samples but I was not there to teach him. [Laughter] I would have been kicked out if I would have done that.

I was very patient with them. When I came there I said I wanted high fire. What they did was fire the biscuit to high fire. They were low fire glazes. It took me forever to glaze just one piece. I got just nuts. They had a big glass spray booth; you were enclosed in that glass. It was hot as anything in New Jersey, you probably know. So, the next year I stamped my feet and said, "It's not worth my while to come here with these, that I want *stoneware* and I want *stoneware glazes*." I got immediately what I wanted without any trouble at all.

The first year [1936] I cannot say I did anything I even liked to look at. It was awful — with their low fire glazes. And they were not pretty low fire glazes. And then Professor Brown got so upset when I would come here to Cranbrook. And he said, "But you have to make your own glazes." And I said, "But that's what I'm interested in."

CRANBROOK

JS: How did your position at Cranbrook start?

MG: They had asked me four times before I came. I felt I did so well in New York and was so independent in New York, I could say, "If I don't want that, I am leaving." I felt if I came to Cranbrook,

everybody would think that it's Professor Saarinen, you see, that has made me. I really felt that I've always had eyes on me from Finland, from everywhere, in that way.

JS: You had known Professor Saarinen from before?

MG: I did not know him. I had met him once briefly.

JS: He knew your work.

MG: Yes. I don't know how it came. I think I had an exhibition here in 1933. I was asked to have an exhibition here and then I was asked to come and teach here. But I did not want to. Once I was in Finland and Mrs. Saarinen was there at the same time in their home there. She invited me over to her and wanted me to come and see her. But I said no, I couldn't, because I'd already contracted with Rutgers. So they kept on trying and I always gave them names that I felt would be good.

JS: Did they have a studio all set up before you came?

MG: They had five wheels and an electric kiln, and a kiln room. That was all. When I fired the electric kiln twice, just testing it, it fired cone 10 at the bottom and cone 014 at the top. [2381-1540°F; 1305-838°C]

When I started to complain about that — I could not fire pottery that way — they said, "Oh, you will learn." I said, "It's because I already have learned that I *know*."

To make a long story short, I told them it's up to me. I cannot get any help from Cranbrook, so I ripped the kiln apart inside and built it differently. I didn't know if it would work; but that's how it has been ever since — even heat.

JS: Was Carl Milles there in 1938 teaching sculpture? [11]

MG: Yes. And everyone said to me, "Do not speak to Carl about ceramic sculpture. Don't you dare speak to him about it." I thought, "Heavens, what is this about?" So the next time I saw him — he wanted us to call him Carl — I said, "What's this that I hear about you that one cannot speak about ceramic sculpture with you?" He said, "Oh, no." And then he told me the story about how he built a kiln in

Sweden and how he almost burned the house down.   It was awful.

A rumor starts and this was just something that somebody had misunderstood.   At that time, it was terrible ceramic sculpture, really. There were very few who did very good ceramic sculpture at that time. I liked Carl Walters[12] very much and Paul Bogatay,[13] but later on; they did not do very much at that time.   There were very few good ones.

JS: Who else was teaching there?

MG: Saarinen was teaching architecture, and Milles sculpture.   But he was not really teaching; you could ask for an appointment.   You could come in that way.   Marshall Fredericks was teaching the sculpture at that time.   The first year Charles Eames was a student and the next year he was teaching design.   And Marianne Strengell,[14] the weaving.

JS: It must have been an exciting place to be in.

MG: I felt I had gotten along so well that I'm going to cocktail parties in New York.   Well, there was nowhere I could not go.   But, again, I started to be afraid to leave New York.   So I felt then it was a good time to move.   You know, if you get too dependent on it…

JS: Is there anything you could say about religion?

MG: I feel all religions.   I mean, I have equal respect for any religion.

[Opens a drawer and offers a clipping from the *American Weekly*. It is Albert Einstein's essay "World View," containing the following excerpt:]

Bowl. *1956. 8⅞×14".
Copper blue pattern and
interior on iron ground.
Syracuse University Art
Collection, 1966.19.*

by Albert Einstein

The first thing we can experience is the mysterious. It is the fundamental emotion which stands at the cradle of true art and true science. Who knows it not, and can no longer feel amazement, is as good as dead, a snuffed-out candle.

A knowledge of the existence of something we cannot penetrate, our perceptions of the profoundest reason and the most radiant beauty, which our minds seem to reach only in their most elementary forms; — it is this knowledge and this emotion that constitute the truly religious attitude: in this sense, and in this alone, I am a deeply religious person.

Enough for me are the mystery of the eternity of life and the inkling of the marvelous structure of reality, together with the single-hearted endeavor to comprehend a portion, be it ever so tiny, of the reason that manifests itself in nature.

The supreme task of the physicist is to arrive at those universal elementary laws from which the cosmos can be built up by pure deduction. The state of mind which enables a person to do work of this kind is akin to that of the religious worshipper or lover; the daily effort comes from no deliberate intention or program, but straight from the heart.

It is the duty of every person of good will to strive steadfastly in their own little world to make the teaching of pure humanity a living force, so far as they can. If they make an honest attempt in this direction without being crushed or trampled underfoot by their contemporaries, they may consider themselves and the community to which they belong lucky.

Bowl. 1942. 3⅝ x 12¼",
The Detroit Institute
of the Arts, 43.85. Founders
Society Purchase,
Kahn Memorial Fund.

1. Charles Fergus Binns (1857-1934). Born in England, trained in ceramic chemistry, first director of the New York College of Clayworking at Alfred, New York, charter member of the American Ceramic Society.

2. Arthur Eugene Baggs (1886-1947). Early student of Professor Binns at Alfred, New York; designer; glaze chemist; teacher and potter; professor at Ohio State University, Columbus, Ohio.

3. Baggs, A.E. & Littlefield, E. "Production and Control of Copper Red Glazes in an Oxidizing Atmosphere," *Journal of the American Ceramic Society*, May 1932, p. 265.

4. Littlefield, Edgar. "Local Reduction Copper Reds," *Ceramics Monthly*, December 1953, p.16.

5. Eliel Saarinen (1873-1950). Leading Finnish architect and teacher, came to the United States in 1923, president of Cranbrook Academy of Art (1932-1946), major projects include the Helsinki Railway Station (1904-1916), Cranbrook (1925-1942), Iowa Art Center (1944-1948).

6. Martha Lauritzen: "I think my most vivid memory of Mr. Eliel Saarinen was his beautiful Sunday attire. He always had snow white pants and shoes, a jacket of American Beauty red, and a white tam."

7. General Motors Technical Center, Warren, Michigan, a complex of buildings designed by Eero Saarinen and Associates (1945-1946).

8. Toini Muona (1904-1987). Studio artist at the Arabia factory, Helsinki (1931-1970), gold medals in Milan (1933), Brussels (1935), Paris (1937). She wrote in 1954: "Clay — you are my dearest friend. When you softly caress my hand, it begins to submit you to my will. Forms emerge one after another. Creative dissatisfaction constantly casts you into new moulds until at last I feel I must break everything down into primary elements and start all over again. That's how you are — my friend the clay." (See Bibliography.)

9. Henry Street Settlement, founded by Lillian Wald in 1893 as a visiting nurse center to serve the immigrant community on New York's lower East Side, expanded to include a full range of social services including an art center which, after over one hundred years, is still going strong.

10. Two sculpture exhibitions at the Brummer Gallery in 1926 and 1933 by Constantin Brancusi (1876-1957) were landmarks in the presentation of modern art from Europe. Two carved wood *Endless Columns* and a plaster *Cock,* however, were cut down in order to fit them into the low-ceilinged space.

11. Carl Milles (1875-1955). Celebrated Swedish sculptor, worked with Rodin, major commissions in Sweden and across the United States.

12. Carl Walters (1883-1955). Painter and ceramic sculptor, widely exhibited.

13. Paul Bogatay (1905-1972). Student of Arthur Baggs, professor at Ohio State University, awarded two first prizes at Syracuse Ceramic National Exhibitions.

14. Marianne Strengell (1909-   ). Internationally-known weaver, teacher, textile designer for industry and architecture. Resident artist and instructor in textiles at Cranbrook 1937-1961. Born in Helsinki.

Opposite: Jar. *16 x 14⅜".*
Photograph courtesy Galerie
Bischofberger, Zurich. Above:
Bowl. *1960. 2¾ x 7½". Porcelain.*
Cranbrook Art Museum, 1970.18.
Photograph by Dirk Bakker.

Opposite: Vase. *1949.*
13¼ x 11½". Syracuse University.
Photograph by Ferdinand Boesch.
Right: Vase. *1947. 20 x 9½".*
Cranbrook Art Museum, 1970.10.
Photograph by Dirk Bakker.

Opposite: Vase. *1951.*
12⅞ x 11 ³⁄₁₆". Cranbrook Art
Museum, 1952.4. Photograph
by Jack Ramsdale. Above: Plate.
1955. 2⅜ x 14". Cranbrook Art
Museum, 1970.27. Photograph
by Dirk Bakker.

Page 76: Vase. *1949. 10½ x 10½".*
American Craft Museum, 1952.4.
Photograph by Ferdinand Boesch.
Page 77: Vase. *1956. 14½ x 12".*
Cranbrook Art Museum,
Gift of Mrs. William Eddy.
Photograph by Ferdinand Boesch.
Above: Bowl. *1951. 5½ x 9¼".*
Cranbrook Art Museum, 1953.8.
Photograph by Ferdinand Boesch.

American Studio Ceramics 1920-1950. Catalog of exhibition. Minneapolis, MN: University Art Museum, University of Minnesota, 1988.

Clark, Garth. *A Century of Ceramics in the United States: 1878-1978: A Study of Its Development.* New York: E. P. Dutton, 1978.

– *American Ceramics: 1876-Present*. Revised Edition. New York: Abbeville Press, 1987.

Clark, Robert Judson et al. *Design in America: The Cranbrook Vision 1925-1950*. New York: Harry N. Abrams, Inc., 1983. Chapter 8, "Ceramics," by Martin Eidelberg, pp. 212-235.

Einstein, Albert. *The World As I See It*. New York, Covici, Friede 1934.

Geist, Sidney. *Brancusi – A Study of the Sculpture*. Grossman, NY 1986

Grotell, Maija. Interview conducted by Jeff Schlanger and Toshiko Takaezu at Cranbrook Academy of Art, Bloomfield Hills, MI, May 24, 1968. ACC Library Collection.

Leach, Bernard. *A Potter's Book*. New York, London: Transatlantic Arts, 1946.

Levin, Elaine. "Maija Grotell — Herbert Sanders," *Ceramics Monthly*, November 1976, pp. 48-54.

–"Maija Grotell," *American Ceramics*, 1/1 Winter 1982, pp. 42-45.

– *History of American Ceramics*. New York: Abrams, pp. 180-181.

Maija Grotell Archives, George Arents Research Library, Syracuse University, Syracuse, NY

Peterson, Susan. *The Craft and Art of Clay*. 2nd Edition. Englewood Cliffs, NJ: Prentice-Hall, 1995.

Schlanger, Jeff. "Maija Grotell." *Craft Horizons*, 29 Nov/Dec. 1969, pp. 15-23.

– "Works Which Grow From Belief." *Form, Function, Finland*. Vol. 3, 1984, pp. 52-56.

Sultz, Phil and Lang, Tom. *Maija Grotell Box*. St. Louis, MO: Singing Bone Press, limited edition, 1985.

Toini Muona. Arabia. 1931-1970. Taideteollisuus Museon Julkaisu (Museum of Applied Arts) No. 27, Helsinki, 1988.

Patterned Plate. 1¼ x 12⅛".
Collection of Margueritte Kimball.
Photograph by Ben E. Watkins.

Born: Helsingfors, Finland August 19, 1899

Graduate of the Central School of Arts and Crafts, Helsinki.

Came to the United States, October 1927.

Instructor at Inwood Pottery Studios, New York, NY, 1927-1928.

Union Settlement, New York, NY, 1928-1929.

Henry Street Settlement, New York, NY, 1929-1938.

Instructor and research assistant, Rutgers University, School
of Ceramic Engineering, New Brunswick, NJ 1936-1938.

Head of the Department of Ceramics, Cranbrook Academy
of Art, Bloomfield Hills, MI, 1938-1966.

Died: Pontiac, Michigan, December 6, 1973.

American Craft Museum, New York, NY

Art Department of the University of Michigan

Art Institute of Chicago, Chicago, IL

Ball State Teachers' College

Central Michigan College of Education

Children's Museum, Detroit, MI

Cleveland Museum of Art, Cleveland, OH

Detroit Institute of Arts, Detroit, MI

Everson Museum of Art, Syracuse, NY

Flint Institute of Art, Flint, MI

Metropolitan Museum of Art, New York, NY

Museum, Cranbrook Academy of Art

Museum of Applied Arts, Helsinki, Finland

Museum of Art, University of Michigan

Sheldon Memorial Art Gallery, University of Nebraska

Springfield Art Museum, Springfield, MO

Syracuse University, Syracuse, NY

The National Gallery, Smithsonian Institution

Toledo Museum of Art, Toledo, OH

University Gallery, Minneapolis, MN

University of Minnesota Art Museum, Minneapolis, MN

Wichita Art Association Gallery, Wichita, KS

Page 82: Vase. *1947.*
17⅜ x 8¼". Ash glaze. University
of Minnesota Art Museum,
Minneapolis, 1953.8. Above:
Bowl. *1943. 8"dia. Copper pink.*
Cranbrook Art Museum, 1952.6.
Photograph by Dirk Bakker.

The International Exposition Barcelona: *Diploma de Colaborador*, 1929.

American Ceramic Society Exposition, Cleveland, OH: Certificate of Excellence, 1931.

Paris International Exposition: Silver Medal, 1937.

The Society of Arts and Crafts, Boston, MA: Honorable Mention, 1935; Elected Master Craftsman, 1938.

The National Ceramic Exhibition, Syracuse Museum of Fine Arts, Syracuse, NY: Second Prize, 1936; Honorable Mention, 1933, 1934, 1941; Encyclopedia Britannica Prize and Special Commendation for Group, 1946; G.R. Croker and Company Prize, 1949.

The Wichita Art Association, Wichita, KS: First Prize, 1947; Purchase Prize, 1951; Honorable Mention, 1954.

The Michigan Artist Craftsman Exhibition: The Lillian Henkel Hass Prize, 1949; The Material and Design Prize, 1950; Mr. and Mrs. Harry L. Winston Prize, 1951; The Founders Society Prize, 1953; Mr. and Mrs. Lawrence A. Fleischman Purchase Prize, 1955.

International Exposition, Cannes: *Diplome D'Honneur*, 1955.

The Michigan Academy of Science, Arts and Letters: Award of Merit of the First Class in the Art of Ceramics, 1949, 1950, 1951, 1956.

The Charles Fergus Binns Medal, Alfred University, Alfred, NY, 1961.

Cranbrook Founders Medal, 1964.

Cranbrook Academy of Art Faculty Medal, 1966.

Executed commissions for General Motors Technical Center and The Cranbrook Foundation; Ceramic Research for Professor Eliel Saarinen.

She liked sitting in Battery Park [New York], looking toward the Narrows, thinking about Finland and the same water touching both shores.

Fred Mitchell

Ostentation and arrogance were not in your vocabulary.

Zoltan Sepeshy

Inscrutable Maija. She said so much with so few words, or perhaps just a glance. Her insightful approach, as a teacher, was of great value, because it made us examine our own resources.

Nancy Plum

Beneath the inscrutable face and quiet manner there was a magnificent strength and a well-fashioned philosophy. She taught by osmosis. You literally absorbed her attitudes.

She rarely criticized directly. Her opinions emerged through small conversations in the studio, but her message always came through. These were some of her messages: You are an important artist. Never undersell yourself. Hard work and sacrifice may be necessary. Research and testing are important. Concentrate on one-of-a-kind objects and exhibit them wholeheartedly.

Mary Kring Risley

Maija's astute, honest, sharp criticism would sometimes fall into place months later, but it was always true. Maija didn't say very much and what she didn't say was as important as what she did say, once you realized that she was thoroughly aware of everything you did.

The realization and acceptance of the rare wordless words in Maija's teaching and being had a strong impact which created the formless form (no alternative but that one has to go inside to form your own form, and that form is to become an individual).

Toshiko Takaezu

Page 82: Vase. *1949-50. 9½ x 9⅞". Collection of Martha Lauritzen. Photograph by Erik Lauritzen.* Opposite: Maija Grotell Box. *1986. Hand-made box with mixed-media contents featuring hand-press printing on assorted papers as well as color reproduction postcards and birch-bark. Produced at Singing Bone Press, St. Louis in an edition of seventy by Phil Sultz with Tom Lang. Photograph by Al Karevy*

To me she was complex, multifaceted, quite inexplicable. To her students, Maija was fun-loving, dedicated, joyous, giving, ever patient, playful, untiring and eminently fair in her critical assessment of others' work. To those beyond the studio door she seemed reclusive, shy, asocial, self-effacing, intensely private and independent.

To herself, she was severely demanding, single-mindedly dedicated and very profligate of her physical energies.

Martha Lauritzen

She was, in my mind, the consummate art teacher. She modeled strong commitment and high personal standards, but never, never imposed her own design outlook on her students. Instead, she truly gave of herself, in so many ways, to help each of us find our own way.

Years later, when my father talked with Shoji Hamada in Japan, mentioning that his son had studied with both Maija Grotell and Marguerite Wildenhain, Hamada pointed to his head and said, "Marguerite," and then to his heart and said "Maija."

Carl Rattner

There was only one word for Maija Grotell: **SISU***

Marianne Strengell

*Finnish for guts, courage, nerve, heart–
the guts of a long-distance runner,
the guts of a long-distance skier.

Bowl. *1959. 3x11".*
Photograph by Peter Lester.

There is a palette of earths
vast as the spectrum of visible light
developed by heat and flame yet
dense as stone.

An artist attempts, in the process
of delivering a human story whole,
to compose feelings into tangible material
form around an object deeply touched.

Beneath the ceramic surface,
within the very substance of your composition,
inspiration and expression,
depth and resonance
may be looked for in time, revealed
eventually by the quality of fire,
traces of texture in the clay
and the transformed residue
of some vibration of passion
in the moment of submission
to the one universal ceramic process.

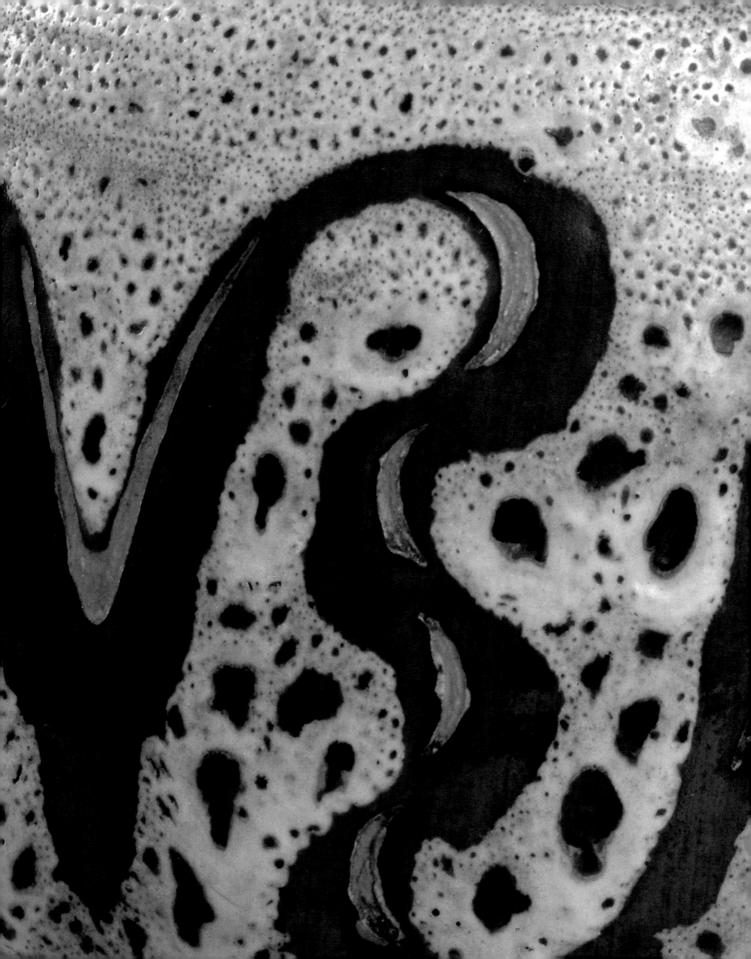

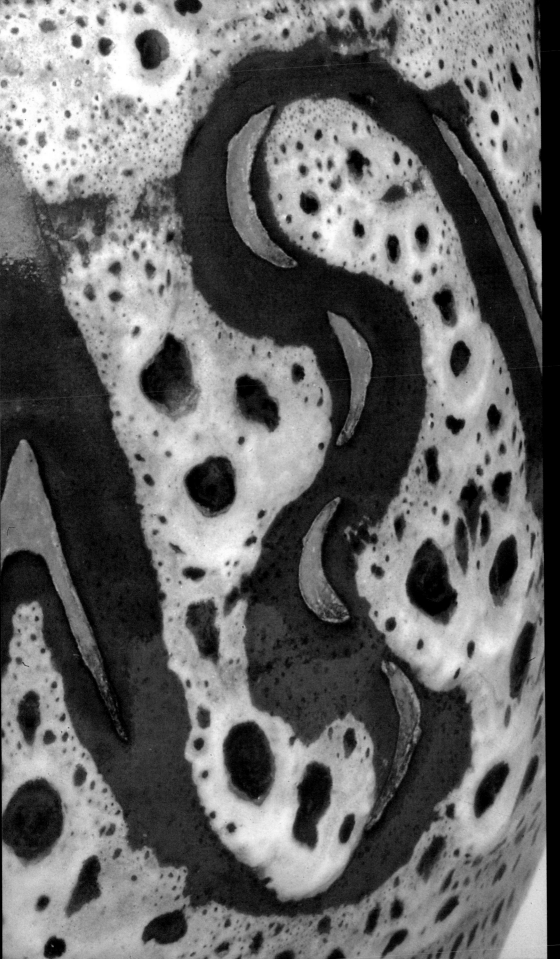

Detail of Vase shown in color on page 86. Production Technique: Jordan clay was thrown on a foot-powered wheel. Over Albany slip, a Bristol glaze was applied by brush onto the damp unfired clay body, both in varying thicknesses to control the sizes of the anticipated crater bubbles. Areas for later glaze inlay were scraped away to expose the clay body. The piece was fired in an electric kiln to cone 10 and cooled for 48 hours. A cone 012 glaze with uranium oxide as a coloring agent was brushed onto the vitrified body in the inlay areas, and the piece was again fired in oxidation to cone 012 to develop the bright orange color.

As authors, we are attempting to be true to Maija's singular voice and stance, as well as to our own reflections together through three decades. For us, this publication is a firing of our understanding, a paper fire offered for the global inspiration of all the turning younger makers of studio pottery.

Practicing ceramic art side-by-side with Toshiko Takaezu while meditating together on the meaning of Maija's art has been at heart an inspiring family experience – like finding a mother and a sister in the clay.

Maija PEACE Shrine kiln, conceived in 1971 and developed through the 1980s and '90s, is a small, glazed-brick building dedicated to the peaceful arts. It is also the place around which my daily working life turns. Its great weight, along with the ongoing rhythms of stacking and unstacking, washing, sweeping and the total engagement necessary to complete each fire, constitutes another embodiment of Maija's legacy. The last of 400 ceramic Faces, called *Nagasaki*, was seen in San Francisco last summer on the 50th anniversary of the Nagasaki bombing, while a ceramic model of Maija PEACE Shrine was set up at the International Museum of Peace in Samarkand. This completes another circle Maija started turning with her strong foot.

Jeff Schlanger

This publication on Maija Grotell is very important and meaningful to me. It is something that has to be done. It is a book that had to be compiled with much care and consideration. Her work and life have much to offer.

In the late 1940s I became aware of the necessity of furthering my understanding of clay. During that period a friend, Amy Russell, who attended Cranbrook Academy of Art and worked with Maija Grotell, gave me a description of the school. I became totally intrigued with Maija's work, which I had seen in a magazine, and also by her signature. It had a special sense of strength and made me want to study with her.

I was apprehensive about being accepted at Cranbrook, but to my surprise I was. This was the beginning of my life as a student of Maija Grotell. Being her student was not simple. To begin with, her teaching was completely different – no specific directions, and criticism was given only when asked for. She made references that were unrelated – yet related. Many times, I didn't feel I could be a potter, but realized the work was important and the opportunities to experiment in this material were vast. Dedication and honesty were vital and helped me to find my own direction and identity.

The highest point in my life was to fulfill my dream of having an exhibition in Japan. It has become a reality. This first exhibition was at the National Museum of Modern Art in Kyoto in June 1995. It will be shown in three other museums. It was important and significant since my parents came from Japan. This exhibition has completed a circle. With each recognition I receive, I feel it was Maija Grotell's teaching that made it possible.

We were fortunate to have had the opportunity to interview Maija. Her willingness to answer all the questions gave us a special insight into her life and work. Jeff and I had a mutual feeling and understanding in the making of this book; dedication, energy and time have made it possible.

Toshiko Takaezu